CONTENTS

Chapter 4: Investing for Wealth

Understanding Different Investment Vehicles

Building a Diversified Investment Portfolio

Risk Management and Asset Allocation

Chapter 5: Passive Income Strategies

Exploring Passive Income Streams

Real Estate Investments and Rental Income

Dividend Stocks and Investment Income

Chapter 6: Entrepreneurship and Business Ventures

Identifying Opportunities for Business Success

Navigating Challenges and Growing a Business

Scaling and Expanding for Higher Profits

Chapter 7: Wealth Protection and Risk Management

Safeguarding Assets and Wealth Preservation

The Importance of Insurance and Estate Planning

Mitigating Financial Risks for Peace of Mind

Chapter 8: The Art of Negotiation and Networking

Developing Effective Negotiation Skills

Building Strong Networks for Opportunities

Collaborating and Partnering for Growth

Chapter 9: Mindfulness and Wealth

Balancing Material Wealth and Well-being

Mindful Spending and Conscious Consumption

Gratitude and Contentment in the Pursuit of Wealth

Chapter 10: Wealth and Happiness

Understanding the Connection between Wealth and Happiness

Cultivating a Balanced and Fulfilling Life

PREFACE

In a world filled with opportunities and potential, **"The Art of Wealth"** offers an inspiring and transformative journey towards financial prosperity and abundance. This book serves as a guiding compass, unveiling the secrets to mastering the path to wealth and fulfillment. By embracing the principles and practices within these pages, readers will gain the tools and wisdom necessary to craft their own unique roadmap to a rich and prosperous life.

Through a holistic perspective, **"The Art of Wealth"** redefines traditional notions of riches, highlighting that true wealth extends far beyond material possessions. A foundation of an abundance mindset is laid, empowering readers to attract prosperity and success into their lives through positive thinking and gratitude.

The book navigates the essential aspects of financial success, commencing with building a robust financial foundation. Budgeting, saving, and eliminating debt become stepping stones towards securing a stable and prosperous future.

Understanding the significance of multiple streams of income, the book dives into diverse investment opportunities such as stocks, real estate, and entrepreneurship. Smart investing strategies are unveiled, empowering readers to take calculated risks and make informed decisions.

Wealth protection and risk management are emphasized as essential pillars of financial security. Readers learn the art of safeguarding assets, securing insurance, and implementing effective estate planning.

The art of negotiation and networking are explored, revealing the power of building strong relationships to unlock boundless opportunities for wealth creation. Collaboration and partnership become catalysts for growth and expansion.

Throughout the book, the significance of financial education is emphasized as a pathway to ongoing growth and prosperity. Readers are encouraged to invest in their knowledge, learning from experts and continuously improving their financial literacy.

At the heart of "**The Art of Wealth**" lies a message of mindfulness and balance. Readers are guided to cultivate a rich and fulfilling life, finding contentment beyond material wealth while maintaining focus on their goals.

The book embraces the concept of giving back and philanthropy, showcasing the profound joy that comes from using wealth to make a positive impact on others' lives. Leaving a legacy of generosity and compassion becomes an integral part of the journey to true prosperity.

Addressing the inevitability of challenges and failures, "The Art of Wealth" offers insights into overcoming obstacles, developing resilience, and growing stronger in the face of adversity.

Above all, "The Art of Wealth" emphasizes that financial prosperity is not an end in itself but rather a means to a life of happiness and fulfillment. As readers embark on their personal journey through these pages, they will discover the keys to unlock their potential, claim their rightful abundance, and create a lasting legacy of wealth and prosperity

CHAPTER 1

WEALTH AND SUCESS

Wealth and success are two intertwined concepts that often go hand in hand but have distinct meanings. Let's explore each concept individually:

1. Wealth: Wealth refers to the abundance of valuable resources, assets, or possessions possessed by an individual, family, or society. It encompasses both tangible and intangible assets, such as money, real estate, investments, valuable possessions, and intellectual property. However, true wealth goes beyond material possessions and includes aspects like knowledge, health, meaningful relationships, and overall well-being

    Key aspects of wealth include:

-   Financial Wealth: The accumulation of monetary assets and resources, allowing for financial security, freedom, and the ability to invest and grow wealth further.

-   Intellectual Wealth: The possession of knowledge, skills, and expertise that can contribute to personal and professional growth, leading to more opportunities for success.

- Health Wealth: The state of physical and mental well-being, which is essential for enjoying life and pursuing one's goals and ambitions.

- Social Wealth: The richness of meaningful relationships, networks, and social connections that can provide support, opportunities, and a sense of belonging.

2. Success: Success is achieving a desired outcome or attaining a set of goals. It can be subjective and may vary from one person to another, as success is often measured based on individual aspirations and values. Success can be experienced in various aspects of life, including career, relationships, personal development, and overall happiness.

Key aspects of success include:

- Professional Success: Achieving career-related goals, such as advancing in one's profession, attaining a specific position, or starting a successful business.

- Personal Success: Fulfillment of personal goals, such as maintaining a healthy lifestyle, nurturing relationships, and finding purpose and happiness.

- Financial Success: The ability to achieve financial stability, manage finances effectively, and achieve financial goals, including wealth accumulation.

- Emotional Success: Developing emotional intelligence, resilience, and the ability to handle challenges and setbacks in a positive and constructive manner.

It is important to note that wealth and success can be interconnected, but they are not synonymous. While wealth often provides opportunities and resources that can contribute to success, true success is not solely measured by material wealth. Success is about achieving a state of contentment, growth, and fulfillment in various areas of life, which can be influenced by both internal and external factors.

Striving for a balanced approach to wealth and success, considering not only material abundance but also personal growth, meaningful connections, and overall well-being, can lead to a truly prosperous and fulfilling life.

Understanding the mindset for getting rich is crucial for achieving financial prosperity and abundance. A wealth-oriented mindset sets the foundation for success by shaping beliefs, attitudes, and behaviors that lead to wealth creation and financial growth. Here are key elements of the mindset for getting rich:

Abundance Mindset: Adopting an abundance mindset involves believing that opportunities for wealth creation are plentiful and that there is enough for everyone. It means focusing on possibilities rather than limitations and being open to new ideas and possibilities.

Positive Thinking: Cultivating a positive attitude towards money, success, and life in general is essential for attracting wealth. Positive thinking helps in overcoming obstacles, staying resilient, and maintaining focus on financial goals.

Goal-Oriented: Setting clear and specific financial goals is a hallmark of a wealth-oriented mindset. Goals provide direction and motivation for taking concrete steps towards wealth accumulation.

Growth Mindset: Embracing a growth mindset means viewing challenges and failures as opportunities for learning and improvement. It involves continuously seeking knowledge and skills to enhance financial intelligence.

Persistence and Determination: A strong mindset for getting rich includes perseverance and a determination to stay committed to financial goals, even in the face of setbacks or obstacles.

Risk Tolerance: Recognizing that wealth-building often involves taking calculated risks and being open to exploring opportunities that may offer higher returns.

Delayed Gratification: Understanding the value of delayed gratification and the importance of making short-term sacrifices for long-term financial gain.

Taking Responsibility: Taking ownership of financial decisions and outcomes, avoiding blame, and proactively seeking solutions.

Surrounding with Like-Minded Individuals: Surrounding oneself with people who have a positive mindset towards money and success can provide support, inspiration, and valuable insights.

Embracing Change: Being adaptable and open to change, as the financial landscape and opportunities continuously evolve.

It is important to note that developing a wealth-oriented mindset is a gradual process that requires self-awareness and consistent effort. Mindset alone is not enough to guarantee wealth, but it lays the groundwork for making informed decisions and taking actions that lead to financial success.

Individuals seeking to get rich should also complement a positive mindset with financial education, effective money management, and strategic investment decisions. Ultimately, it is the combination of the right mindset and practical knowledge that can pave the way to financial prosperity and abundance

CHAPTER 2

BUDGETTING AND SAVING

Budgeting and saving are essential financial habits that lay the foundation for a secure and prosperous future. Budgeting involves carefully tracking income and expenses, creating a plan to allocate money wisely, and living within one's means. It provides a clear overview of where money is going and allows for informed financial decisions. By identifying areas where spending can be reduced and setting financial goals, budgeting helps individuals prioritize their financial objectives.

Saving, on the other hand, is the deliberate act of setting aside money for future needs or investment opportunities. It serves as a safety net during emergencies and unforeseen circumstances, reducing the reliance on credit and debt when unexpected expenses arise. Additionally, saving regularly and consistently contributes to wealth building. Accumulating savings over time enables individuals to invest in assets that grow in value and generate passive income, providing greater financial security and the potential for long-term financial freedom.

Together, budgeting and saving instill financial discipline and responsibility. They empower individuals to take control of their financial well-being, make informed decisions, and pursue their financial goals proactively. By practicing these habits, individuals can achieve financial stability, reach their aspirations, and build a stronger financial future for themselves and their families.

Budgeting and saving are two crucial financial habits that play a significant role in achieving financial stability, building wealth, and securing a more prosperous future. Here are some key reasons why budgeting and saving are important:

1. Financial Control: Budgeting helps you gain better control over your finances. By tracking your income and expenses, you can identify areas where you may be overspending and make necessary adjustments to stay within your means.

2. Debt Management: Budgeting allows you to allocate funds to pay off debts systematically. By managing debt effectively, you can reduce interest payments and work towards becoming debt-free.

3. Savings for Emergencies: Having an emergency fund through saving ensures you have funds set aside for unexpected expenses like medical emergencies, car repairs, or job loss. This financial cushion provides peace of mind and prevents you from falling into debt during difficult times.

4. Achieving Financial Goals: Budgeting helps you prioritize and allocate funds to meet specific financial goals, such as saving for a down payment on a home, funding education, or building a retirement nest egg.

5. Building Wealth: Saving regularly and investing wisely are the cornerstones of wealth building. By consistently saving a portion of your income and making strategic investments, you can grow your net worth over time.

6. Financial Discipline: Budgeting instills financial discipline and helps curb impulsive spending. It encourages responsible money management and helps you resist unnecessary expenses.

7. Planning for Retirement: Budgeting and saving contribute to funding your retirement. By starting early and consistently contributing to retirement accounts, you can enjoy financial security during your golden years.

8. Handling Life Transitions: Budgeting and saving prepare you for life transitions, such as starting a family, purchasing a home, or changing careers. Having financial reserves allows you to navigate these transitions more smoothly.

9. Reduced Stress: Knowing that you have a financial plan and savings can reduce financial stress and anxiety. It provides a sense of financial security and allows you to focus on other aspects of your life with peace of mind.

10. Financial Independence: By budgeting and saving, you can work towards achieving financial independence, where your passive income from investments covers your living expenses, giving you more freedom and flexibility in your life choices.

In conclusion, budgeting and saving are fundamental financial practices that empower you to take control of your financial life, achieve goals, build wealth, and ultimately enjoy greater financial security and peace of mind. By developing these habits early on and consistently following them, you can pave the way to a more prosperous and fulfilling future.

Effective savings and investing

Effective savings and investments are the pillars of financial success and long-term prosperity. Saving money is the foundation of a sound financial plan, providing a safety net for emergencies and unexpected expenses. It involves consistently setting aside a portion of income, regardless of the amount, to build a financial cushion. Effective saving habits also encourage disciplined spending, helping individuals avoid impulsive purchases and unnecessary debts.

On the other hand, investments are crucial for wealth building and achieving financial goals. Investing involves putting money into assets that have the potential to grow in value over time, such as stocks, bonds, real estate, or mutual funds. Effective investing requires careful research, diversification, and a long-term perspective. By harnessing the power of compounding and allowing investments to grow steadily, individuals can create a source of passive income and secure their financial future.

The combination of effective savings and investments creates a virtuous cycle. Saving enables individuals to have funds available to invest, while successful investments yield returns that can be reinvested or used to further financial objectives. This synergy amplifies wealth-building potential and accelerates progress toward financial freedom.

Ultimately, effective savings and investments provide financial security, open doors to opportunities, and allow individuals to realize their dreams and aspirations. Building a robust financial portfolio through disciplined saving and strategic investing empowers individuals to weather financial challenges, attain financial independence, and create a legacy of financial well-being for themselves and future generations

Distinguishing needs from wants

Distinguishing needs from wants is a crucial skill in making sound financial decisions and managing personal finances effectively. Needs are essential for survival and are necessary for maintaining a basic standard of living, while wants are desires or preferences that enhance our lifestyle but are not essential for survival. Here are the key differences between needs and wants:

Necessity: Needs are the fundamental requirements for human survival, such as food, water, shelter, clothing, and healthcare.

Universal: Most needs are universal and apply to all individuals regardless of their circumstances or preferences.

Non-negotiable: Needs are non-negotiable expenses that must be fulfilled to maintain a minimum quality of life.

Limited: The number of needs is relatively limited, and they generally remain constant over time.

Examples of Needs:

- Nutritious food and clean water

- Safe and suitable housing

- Basic clothing appropriate for the climate

- Necessary medical care and medication

- Transportation for work or essential activities

Wants:

1. Desirability: Wants are things that individuals desire or wish to have but are not essential for survival or well-being.

2. Subjective: Wants vary from person to person based on their preferences, interests, and lifestyle choices.

3. Flexible: Wants can change over time or with changes in personal circumstances and preferences.

4. Unlimited: There is a vast array of wants, and new desires may continually emerge as personal preferences evolve.

Examples of Wants:

- Dining out at fancy restaurants

- Owning the latest electronic gadgets

- Luxury vacations and travel experiences

- Designer clothing and accessories

- Entertainment and leisure activities

Distinguishing needs from wants is critical in budgeting and money management. By prioritizing needs over wants, individuals can allocate their financial resources more effectively, ensuring that essential expenses are covered before spending on non-essential items. This approach helps individuals avoid unnecessary debt and financial stress while working towards their long-term financial goals and building a strong financial foundation. Recognizing the difference between needs and wants allows for more conscious spending and paves the way for a more secure and fulfilling financial future

CHAPTER 3

BUILDING A SOLID FINANCIAL FOUNDATION

Eliminating Debt and Managing credit

Eliminating debt and managing credit are integral components of sound financial management. Reducing and eliminating debt is essential for achieving financial freedom and minimizing financial stress. Developing a plan to pay off debts systematically, starting with high-interest debts, helps individuals regain control of their finances. By making regular and larger-than-minimum payments, individuals can accelerate the debt payoff process and save money on interest charges.

Effective debt management also involves avoiding taking on new debts and using credit responsibly. Understanding the terms and conditions of credit cards and loans, as well as the implications of missed payments or high credit utilization, is crucial. Maintaining a good credit score through timely payments and responsible credit usage opens doors to better loan terms and interest rates when seeking new credit or financing options.

Creating a budget and tracking expenses can help identify areas where spending can be reduced to allocate more funds towards debt repayment. Building an emergency fund is another crucial aspect of debt elimination and credit management, as it provides a financial safety net, reducing the reliance on credit during unexpected situations.

Furthermore, seeking professional advice from financial counselors or credit experts can offer personalized guidance and support in developing a debt elimination and credit management strategy. With discipline, perseverance, and a commitment to financial well-being, individuals can work towards a debt-free future and achieve greater financial stability. Managing credit responsibly ensures a healthier financial profile and positions individuals for a more secure and prosperous financial future.

Creating a budget for financial control

Creating a budget is a fundamental step towards achieving financial control and managing money effectively. A budget provides a clear overview of income and expenses, helping individuals make informed financial decisions and stay on track with their financial goals. Here are the steps to create a budget for financial control:

1. Assess Your Finances: Begin by evaluating your current financial situation. Gather information about your income, including your salary, bonuses, and any other sources of income.

2. Track Expenses: Record all your expenses over a specific period, such as a month. Categorize expenses into fixed (e.g., rent, mortgage, utilities) and variable (e.g., groceries, entertainment) to identify where most of your money is going.

3. Set Financial Goals: Define your short-term and long-term financial goals. These goals could include paying off debt, saving for a down payment, creating an emergency fund, or investing for retirement.

4. Allocate Income: Based on your income and expense tracking, allocate funds to cover essential needs first, such as housing, utilities, food, and debt payments. Then, allocate funds for your financial goals and discretionary spending.

5. Prioritize Savings: Make savings a priority in your budget. Allocate a portion of your income to savings and investments before considering discretionary spending.

6. Create Categories: Organize your budget into categories that align with your expenses, such as housing, transportation, groceries, entertainment, debt repayment, and savings.

7. Be Realistic: Ensure that your budget is realistic and achievable. Avoid overestimating income or underestimating expenses, as this could lead to unrealistic expectations.

8. Review Regularly: Revisit and update your budget regularly to reflect changes in income, expenses, or financial goals. Adjust your budget as needed to stay on track with your financial objectives.

9. Use Budgeting Tools: Utilize budgeting tools, apps, or spreadsheets to help you track expenses, analyze spending patterns, and monitor progress towards your financial goals.

10. Be Flexible: Be prepared to make adjustments to your budget when necessary. Life circumstances may change, and flexibility in budgeting can help you adapt to unexpected situations.

By creating a budget, you gain a comprehensive understanding of your financial situation, identify areas where you can save money, and take control of your finances. Budgeting empowers you to make informed choices, avoid overspending, and work towards financial stability and success. With discipline and consistent budget management, you can achieve greater financial control and build a solid foundation for a more secure and prosperous future.

Saving for Emergencies and future investment

Saving for emergencies and future investments are two crucial aspects of financial planning that contribute to long-term financial security and wealth-building. Let's explore each of these components:

1. Saving for Emergencies: Building an emergency fund is a foundational step in financial preparedness. An emergency fund is a savings buffer specifically designated to cover unexpected expenses or financial hardships, such as medical emergencies, car repairs, job loss, or any unforeseen events. Having an emergency fund ensures that you do not need to rely on credit cards or loans during difficult times, preventing additional debt and financial stress.

Key points about saving for emergencies:

- Aim for Adequate Coverage: Typically, an emergency fund should cover three to six months' worth of essential living expenses. The exact amount depends on individual circumstances, such as job stability, family size, and other financial resources.

- Consistent Contributions: Regularly contribute to your emergency fund until it reaches the desired level. You can set up automatic transfers to ensure consistent savings.

- Easy Accessibility: Keep the emergency fund in a liquid and easily accessible account, such as a savings account or a money market fund, so you can quickly access the funds when needed.

2. Saving for Future Investment: Saving for future investments involves setting aside funds to grow wealth over the long term. These investments can include retirement accounts (e.g., 401(k), IRA), brokerage accounts, real estate, and other assets that have the potential to appreciate in value.

Key points about saving for future investments:

- Diversification: Spread your investments across various asset classes to reduce risk. Diversification helps protect your portfolio from significant losses if one particular asset class underperforms.

- Long-Term Perspective: Many investments require time to grow significantly. Adopting a long-term perspective and staying patient can yield better returns and mitigate the impact of short-term market fluctuations.

- Regular Contributions: Make consistent contributions to your investment accounts. Dollar-cost averaging, which involves investing a fixed amount at regular intervals, can help average out market volatility and potentially enhance returns.

- Review and Adjust: Periodically review your investment portfolio to ensure it aligns with your risk tolerance and financial goals. Rebalance your portfolio as needed to maintain the desired asset allocation.

By prioritizing both emergency savings and future investments, you can build a solid financial foundation while working towards long-term financial freedom. Having an emergency fund provides peace of mind during unforeseen circumstances, and disciplined investing can lead to substantial wealth accumulation over time. Combining these two strategies sets you on a path to achieve your financial aspirations and secure a brighter financial future.

CHAPTER 4

INVESTING FOR WEALTH

Understanding Different Investment Vehicles

Understanding different investment vehicles is essential for making informed decisions and building a diversified investment portfolio. Investment vehicles refer to the various options available for individuals to invest their money with the aim of generating returns and building wealth. Each investment vehicle comes with its own risk and return characteristics. Here are some common types of investment vehicles:

Stocks: Stocks represent ownership shares in a company. When you buy a stock, you become a shareholder and have a claim on the company's assets and earnings. Stocks offer the potential for high returns but also come with higher volatility and risk.

Bonds: Bonds are debt securities issued by governments or corporations. When you buy a bond, you are essentially lending money to the issuer in exchange for periodic interest payments and the return of the principal amount at maturity. Bonds generally offer lower returns than stocks but are considered less risky

.

Mutual Funds: Mutual funds pool money from multiple investors to invest in a diversified portfolio of stocks, bonds, or other securities. They are managed by professional fund managers, offering investors diversification and professional expertise.

Exchange-Traded Funds (ETFs): ETFs are similar to mutual funds but trade on stock exchanges like individual stocks. They offer diversification and liquidity and can track various market indexes or sectors.

Real Estate Investment Trusts (REITs): REITs are companies that own or finance income-generating real estate properties, such as office buildings, apartments, or shopping centers. Investing in REITs allows individuals to participate in real estate without directly owning properties.

Certificates of Deposit (CDs): CDs are time deposits offered by banks with fixed terms and interest rates. They are low-risk investments, but funds are locked in for a specific period.

Commodities: Commodities include physical assets like gold, silver, oil, or agricultural products. Investors can trade commodities through futures contracts or ETFs.

Retirement Accounts: Retirement accounts like 401(k)s and Individual Retirement Accounts (IRAs) offer tax advantages to encourage long-term savings for retirement. They can hold a variety of investment options, including stocks, bonds, and mutual funds.

Crypto currencies: Crypto currencies are digital or virtual currencies that use cryptography for security. Bit coin and Ethereum are examples of crypto currencies, and they are known for their high volatility and speculative nature.

Peer-to-Peer Lending: In peer-to-peer lending, individuals lend money to others through online platforms, earning interest on the loans.

Understanding the risk, return potential, and suitability of each investment vehicle is crucial. Diversifying across different investment types can help manage risk and optimize returns. Investors should consider their financial goals, risk tolerance, and investment time horizon when choosing investment vehicles that align with their needs and objectives. Seeking advice from financial advisors can be beneficial in developing a well-balanced and personalized investment strategy.

Building a solid Financial Foundation

Building a solid financial foundation is the cornerstone of achieving long-term financial stability and prosperity. It involves adopting prudent financial habits, making informed decisions, and planning for the future. At its core, a solid financial foundation consists of several key elements.

Firstly, creating and sticking to a budget is essential. A budget helps individuals track income and expenses, prioritize savings, and avoid overspending. By living within their means and consistently saving a portion of their income, individuals can build an emergency fund, providing a safety net for unexpected financial challenges.

Secondly, eliminating high-interest debt is crucial. Paying off debts systematically, starting with those carrying the highest interest rates, frees up financial resources and reduces interest payments over time. Debt elimination is a crucial step in achieving financial freedom.

Thirdly, a solid financial foundation involves investing wisely. Diversifying investments across different asset classes and maintaining a long-term perspective can help grow wealth steadily while managing risk.

Furthermore, adequate insurance coverage, such as health insurance, life insurance, and disability insurance, is vital to protect against unforeseen circumstances that could have devastating financial consequences.

Finally, building a solid financial foundation requires continuous education and learning about personal finance and investment strategies. Being informed empowers individuals to make sound financial decisions and adapt to changing economic conditions.

By integrating these components, individuals can build a robust financial foundation that provides security, flexibility, and a pathway to achieve their financial goals. Establishing a strong financial base allows for greater peace of mind, confidence in handling financial challenges, and the ability to pursue opportunities for growth and wealth-building. Ultimately, a solid financial foundation lays the groundwork for a more secure and prosperous future.

Risk management and Asset Allocation

Risk management and asset allocation are two critical components of a well-rounded investment strategy. They play pivotal roles in achieving financial goals while managing potential risks.

Risk management involves identifying, assessing, and mitigating potential risks that could impact an investment portfolio. Different types of risks, such as market risk, inflation risk, credit risk, and geopolitical risk, can affect the performance of investments. By diversifying investments across various asset classes, industries, and geographic regions, investors can reduce the impact of individual risks on their overall portfolio. Additionally, setting a risk tolerance level helps investors maintain a disciplined approach during periods of market volatility and avoid making impulsive decisions based on short-term fluctuations.

Asset allocation, on the other hand, refers to the process of dividing an investment portfolio among different asset classes, such as stocks, bonds, cash, and real estate. The goal of asset allocation is to achieve a balance between potential return and risk that aligns with the investor's financial objectives, time horizon, and risk tolerance. A well-considered asset allocation takes into account factors such as age, financial goals, income, and risk appetite.

Both risk management and asset allocation are dynamic processes. As an investor's circumstances change or market conditions fluctuate, adjustments to the portfolio may be necessary to maintain the desired risk-return profile. Regular reviews and rebalancing of the portfolio can ensure that it remains aligned with the investor's long-term financial goals.

By combining effective risk management practices with a thoughtfully designed asset allocation strategy, investors can enhance the potential for achieving their financial objectives while mitigating the impact of market fluctuations and unexpected events. This approach fosters greater confidence in one's investment decisions and reinforces a long-term perspective, fostering financial security and success.

CHAPTER 5

PASSIVE INCOME STRATEGIES

Exploring passive income streams

Passive income streams refer to sources of income that require little to no ongoing effort or active involvement once they are set up. Unlike traditional active income, where you exchange time and effort for money, passive income allows you to earn money with minimal ongoing work. Here are some common passive income streams worth exploring:

1. Rental Properties: Owning and renting out real estate properties, such as apartments, houses, or commercial spaces, can generate rental income. Property management companies can handle day-to-day operations, making it a relatively passive source of income.

2. Dividend Stocks: Investing in dividend-paying stocks allows you to earn regular dividends without actively

managing the investments. Companies share a portion of their profits with shareholders through dividends.

3. Royalties: If you create and own intellectual property, such as books, music, or artwork, you can earn royalties from its usage or sale without ongoing work.

4. Peer-to-Peer Lending: Peer-to-peer lending platforms enable you to lend money to individuals or businesses in exchange for interest payments, providing passive income over time.

5. High-Yield Savings Accounts or CDs: Although the returns may be modest, placing money in high-yield savings accounts or Certificates of Deposit (CDs) can generate passive interest income.

6. Real Estate Crowd funding: Invest in real estate projects through crowd funding platforms, where you can earn returns from rental income or property appreciation.

7. Affiliate Marketing: By promoting products or services through affiliate programs, you can earn commissions on sales generated through your referral links.

8. Automated Online Businesses: Creating and automating online businesses, such as e-commerce stores or digital products, can generate passive income when sales are made without your direct involvement.

9. License Your Photos or Videos: If you are a photographer or videographer, you can license your work to stock photo or video platforms, earning passive income whenever someone purchases or downloads your content.

10. Create Online Courses or E-books: Developing online courses or e-books allows you to earn passive income from sales, especially if the content continues to be relevant and valuable over time.

It's essential to note that creating passive income streams often requires initial effort, time, and sometimes financial investment. Additionally, maintaining and growing these income streams may still require periodic attention. However, the potential to earn money with reduced ongoing effort makes passive income an attractive addition to one's financial strategy, helping individuals achieve financial freedom and diversify their income sources

Real Estate Investments and Rental Income

Real estate investments and rental income are popular and lucrative avenues for building wealth and generating passive income. Real estate investment involves acquiring properties with the intention of earning a return on investment through rental income and property appreciation. Here's an overview of real estate investments and rental income:

1. Real Estate Investments: Real estate investments come in various forms, including residential properties (e.g., houses, apartments), commercial properties (e.g., office buildings, retail spaces), and industrial properties (e.g., warehouses). Investors can choose to buy properties directly or invest in real estate through real estate investment trusts (REITs) or real estate crowd funding platforms.

2. Rental Income: Rental income is the money earned from tenants who occupy the investment property. Property owners can lease out residential or commercial spaces to individuals or businesses, earning monthly rent payments.

Rental income can provide a steady stream of cash flow and potentially cover property-related expenses, such as mortgage payments, property taxes, and maintenance costs.

Benefits of Real Estate Investments and Rental Income:

1. Passive Income: Rental income offers a passive income stream, providing ongoing cash flow without requiring daily involvement in the business.

2. Diversification: Real estate investments can diversify a portfolio, reducing reliance on traditional investments like stocks and bonds.

3. Property Appreciation: Over time, real estate properties may increase in value, providing potential capital appreciation and building equity.

4. Tax Benefits: Real estate investors may enjoy tax advantages, including depreciation deductions, mortgage interest deductions, and the ability to defer capital gains through 1031 exchanges (in some regions).

5. Inflation Hedge: Real estate investments can act as a hedge against inflation, as property values and rental income tend to increase with inflation.

Challenges of Real Estate Investments and Rental Income:

1. Property Management: Managing rental properties can be time-consuming and may require dealing with tenant issues, property maintenance, and legal obligations.

2. Market Risks: Real estate values can fluctuate due to changes in the local housing market or economic conditions, affecting property appreciation potential.

3. Vacancies and Cash Flow: Rental income may fluctuate depending on vacancies and tenant turnover, impacting cash flow.

4. Initial Capital and Financing: Acquiring real estate properties often requires significant upfront capital and securing financing, which can be a barrier for some investors.

Successful real estate investments and rental income require careful research, due diligence, and a comprehensive understanding of local real estate markets. Engaging property managers or real estate investment companies can help ease the burden of property management for investors seeking more hands-off approaches to real estate investments. By leveraging rental income and potential property appreciation, real estate investments can be an effective strategy to create long-term wealth and financial stability.

Dividend Stocks and Investment Income

Dividend stocks are a type of equity investment in which shareholders receive a portion of the company's profits in the form of regular dividend payments. Dividends are typically distributed by well-established and financially stable companies as a way to reward shareholders for their investment and attract long-term investors. Investing in dividend stocks can provide a consistent stream of investment income, making them a popular choice for income-oriented investors. Here's an overview of dividend stocks and their role in generating investment income:

1. Dividend Stocks: Dividend stocks are shares of publicly traded companies that have a history of paying regular dividends to their shareholders. These companies are often mature and have a stable business model, generating sufficient profits to distribute a portion of those profits back to investors. Dividend stocks are typically found in sectors such as utilities, consumer staples, financial services, and healthcare.

2. Investment Income: Investment income from dividend stocks is the money received by shareholders in the form of dividend payments. Dividends are usually paid on a per-share basis and can be distributed quarterly, semi-annually, or annually. The amount of dividend income depends on the number of shares owned and the dividend yield, which is the annual dividend amount as a percentage of the stock's current price.

Benefits of Dividend Stocks and Investment Income:

1. Steady Income Stream: Dividend payments provide a steady and predictable income stream, making them particularly attractive for investors seeking regular cash flow.

2. Diversification: Including dividend stocks in an investment portfolio can add diversification, complementing other investment types like growth stocks or bonds.

3. Lower Risk: Companies that pay dividends are often well-established and financially stable, reducing the investment risk compared to speculative stocks.

4. Potential for Growth: Some dividend-paying companies may increase their dividends over time, providing potential for income growth and capital appreciation.

5. Tax Advantages: In some regions, dividend income may be subject to lower tax rates than other types of investment income, making them tax-efficient for certain investors.

Challenges of Dividend Stocks and Investment Income:

Market Volatility: Dividend stocks are still subject to market fluctuations, and the stock price can change based on company performance and economic conditions.

Dividend Cuts: Companies may reduce or eliminate dividends during challenging economic times or if they face financial difficulties.

Limited Growth Potential: While dividend stocks can provide steady income, their growth potential may be lower compared to growth-oriented investments.

Dividend stocks can play an essential role in an income-focused investment strategy, especially for investors seeking regular income without needing to sell assets. However, it's crucial to carefully assess dividend stocks, considering factors like the company's financial health, dividend history, and overall portfolio diversification. Investors should align their investment choices with their financial goals, risk tolerance, and time horizon to build a well-balanced investment portfolio.

CHAPTER 6

ENTREPRENEURSHIP AND BUSINESS VENTURES

Identifying Opportunities for Business Success

Identifying opportunities for business success is a vital aspect of entrepreneurship and strategic planning. It involves recognizing potential areas where a business can thrive, grow, and achieve its objectives. Successful businesses proactively seek and capitalize on opportunities that align with their strengths, market demands, and industry trends. Here are key elements in identifying opportunities for business success:

Market Research: Conducting comprehensive market research is fundamental to identifying opportunities. Understanding customer needs, preferences, and pain points allows businesses to tailor their products or services to meet market demands effectively.

Competitive Analysis: Analyzing competitors' strengths and weaknesses can reveal gaps in the market that a business can fill or innovative ways to differentiate from rivals.

Technology and Innovation: Embracing technology and fostering a culture of innovation enables businesses to create novel solutions and stay ahead in a rapidly evolving marketplace.

Changing Consumer Behavior: Identifying shifts in consumer behavior and emerging trends can lead to new opportunities, such as offering eco-friendly products or catering to digital-savvy customers.

1. Industry Trends: Staying informed about industry trends and disruptions enables businesses to adapt and take advantage of emerging opportunities.

2. Partnerships and Collaborations: Forming strategic partnerships or collaborations with other businesses can open doors to new markets, resources, and expertise.

3. Global Expansion: Exploring opportunities in international markets can enable businesses to tap into new customer bases and diversify revenue streams.

4. Customer Feedback: Listening to customer feedback and incorporating it into business strategies can lead to product improvements and increased customer satisfaction.

5. Regulatory Changes: Understanding and adapting to changing regulations can create opportunities for businesses to address new demands or compliance requirements.

6. Social and Environmental Responsibility: Embracing corporate social responsibility and sustainability initiatives can attract socially-conscious customers and investors.

Businesses that actively seek and capitalize on opportunities have a greater chance of achieving sustainable growth and success. Flexibility, agility, and a forward-thinking mindset are essential attributes for businesses to seize opportunities and navigate challenges effectively. Identifying opportunities for business success requires a proactive and adaptive approach, coupled with a deep understanding of the market, industry dynamics, and customer needs. By staying vigilant and open to innovation, businesses can position themselves for long-term prosperity in a dynamic and competitive business landscape.

Navigating Challenges and Growing a Business

Navigating challenges and achieving growth is an inherent part of building and sustaining a successful business. Whether it's a startup or an established company, every business faces various obstacles and opportunities for growth. Here are some key strategies for effectively navigating challenges and fostering business growth:

1. Embrace Adaptability: The business landscape is constantly changing, and successful businesses must be adaptable. Stay open to new ideas, technologies, and market trends, and be willing to adjust your business strategies accordingly.

2. Customer-Centric Approach: Focus on understanding your customers' needs and preferences. Use customer feedback to improve products or services and build lasting relationships with clients.

3. Continuous Innovation: Innovation is critical for staying competitive. Encourage a culture of innovation within your

organization, rewarding and nurturing creative ideas that can lead to breakthrough solutions.

4. Strong Leadership: Effective leadership is essential for guiding a business through challenges and inspiring employees to work towards common goals. Lead by example and communicate a clear vision for the future.

5. Strategic Planning: Develop a well-defined business plan that outlines short-term and long-term goals, along with strategies to achieve them. Regularly review and update the plan to adapt to changing circumstances.

6. Build a Skilled Team: Surround yourself with talented and motivated employees who align with your business's values and goals. Invest in training and professional development to nurture a skilled workforce.

7. Financial Management: Maintain a robust financial management system. Monitor cash flow, control expenses, and seek opportunities for cost savings to ensure financial stability.

8. Market and Competitor Analysis: Stay informed about the market landscape and your competitors. Understanding your position relative to competitors can help you identify areas for improvement and differentiation.

9. Customer Acquisition and Retention: Focus on both acquiring new customers and retaining existing ones. Implement effective marketing strategies to attract new clients, and provide exceptional customer service to build loyalty.

10. Risk Management: Identify and address potential risks that could impact your business. Develop contingency plans to mitigate the effects of unexpected challenges.

11. Network and Collaborate: Engage with other businesses, industry peers, and professional networks. Collaborative relationships can lead to partnerships, shared knowledge, and new business opportunities.

12. Celebrate Success and Learn from Failures: Acknowledge and celebrate achievements along the way. At the same time, view failures as learning opportunities to improve and grow stronger.

By combining these strategies with resilience, determination, and a customer-focused mindset, businesses can effectively navigate challenges and foster sustained growth. Embrace change, learn from experiences, and continuously seek opportunities to innovate and evolve. Through strategic planning, adaptability, and a commitment to excellence, businesses can thrive in the face of challenges and achieve lasting success.

Scaling and Expanding for Higher Profits

Scaling and expanding a business is a strategic approach that aims to increase revenue, market presence, and profitability. It involves growing the business beyond its current capacity to capitalize on market opportunities and generate higher profits. Here are key strategies for scaling and expanding a business for higher profits:

1. Market Research and Analysis: Conduct thorough market research to identify new opportunities, emerging trends,

and underserved customer segments. Understanding market dynamics is essential for making informed expansion decisions.

2. Streamlined Operations: Optimize business processes and operations to enhance efficiency and reduce costs. Automate tasks, improve supply chain management, and implement lean practices to free up resources for growth initiatives.

3. Innovation and Product Development: Continuously innovate and develop new products or services that address customer needs and preferences. Offering unique and improved solutions can attract a broader customer base and increase profits.

4. Geographic Expansion: Consider entering new geographic markets where there is demand for your products or services. Expanding to new regions can provide access to a larger customer pool and diversify revenue streams.

5. Strategic Partnerships: Form strategic partnerships or alliances with complementary businesses. Collaborating with other companies can enable access to new markets, resources, and distribution channels.

6. Online Presence and E-commerce: Embrace digital transformation and establish a robust online presence. E-commerce platforms can significantly expand the reach of a business, reaching customers globally.

7. Customer Retention and Loyalty: Prioritize customer retention and focus on building customer loyalty. Satisfied and loyal customers are more likely to make repeat purchases and refer others, increasing profits.

8. Scaling Marketing and Sales Efforts: Invest in marketing and sales activities to increase brand awareness and customer acquisition. Implement targeted marketing campaigns and expand sales channels to reach a wider audience.

9. Strong Financial Management: Maintain sound financial management practices. Monitor cash flow, manage debt responsibly, and allocate resources strategically to support growth initiatives.

10. Talent Acquisition and Development: Build a skilled and motivated workforce to support business expansion. Invest in talent acquisition, training, and development to ensure the organization has the capabilities to scale effectively.

11. Acquisitions and Mergers: Consider acquisitions or mergers with other companies to accelerate growth and gain a competitive advantage in the market.

12. Customer Feedback and Adaptation: Listen to customer feedback and adapt your products, services, and business strategies accordingly. Customer insights can guide improvements and enhance profitability.

Successful scaling and expansion require careful planning, adequate resources, and a clear vision for the future. It is essential to strike a balance between ambitious growth goals and sustainable business practices. Continuously monitor progress, adjust strategies as needed, and maintain a customer-centric approach to achieve higher profits and long-term success.

CHAPTER 7

WEALTH PROTECTION AND RISK MANAGEMNT

Safe Guarding Assets and Wealth Preservation

Safeguarding assets and wealth preservation are crucial aspects of financial planning and risk management. Protecting assets ensures that they are shielded from potential threats, such as market volatility, lawsuits, or unforeseen financial challenges. Wealth preservation focuses on maintaining the value and purchasing power of assets over time to secure financial stability and achieve long-term financial goals. Here are key strategies for safeguarding assets and wealth preservation:

1. Diversification: Diversifying investments across different asset classes can reduce the impact of market fluctuations on the overall portfolio. A well-diversified portfolio can help mitigate risks and preserve wealth.

2. Insurance Coverage: Adequate insurance coverage, including home insurance, car insurance, health insurance, and liability insurance, protects assets and mitigates potential financial losses from unexpected events.

3. Estate Planning: Developing a comprehensive estate plan, including wills, trusts, and power of attorney, ensures that assets are distributed according to your wishes and minimizes estate taxes.

4. Asset Protection Strategies: Utilize legal structures, such as limited liability companies (LLCs) or trusts, to protect personal and business assets from potential lawsuits or creditor claims.

5. Risk Management: Identify potential risks that could impact assets and implement risk management strategies to minimize exposure to those risks.

6. Regular Financial Review: Conduct regular reviews of your financial situation to assess asset performance, adjust investment strategies, and ensure alignment with financial goals.

7. Long-Term Focus: Adopt a long-term perspective in financial decisions, avoiding short-term speculation and focusing on sustainable wealth preservation.

8. Emergency Fund: Maintain an emergency fund to cover unexpected expenses and provide a financial buffer during times of economic uncertainty.

9. Professional Advice: Seek advice from financial advisors, estate planners, and legal experts to develop a customized wealth preservation strategy that aligns with your specific needs and goals.

10. Continual Education: Stay informed about changes in tax laws, regulations, and financial markets to make informed decisions and adapt wealth preservation strategies accordingly.

By implementing these strategies, individuals and families can protect their assets, minimize financial risks, and preserve wealth for future generations. Safeguarding assets and wealth preservation are integral components of a comprehensive financial plan, providing peace of mind and the foundation for a secure financial future.

Importance of Insurance and Estate planning

Insurance and estate planning are critical components of a comprehensive financial strategy, providing protection, security, and peace of mind for individuals and their families. Let's explore the importance of each:

1. Importance of Insurance:

- Risk Mitigation: Insurance provides financial protection against various risks, such as accidents, illnesses, natural disasters, and liability claims. It ensures that individuals and families are financially covered during challenging and unexpected situations.

- Asset Protection: Insurance safeguards valuable assets, such as homes, cars, and businesses, from potential damage or loss, reducing the financial burden of replacing or repairing these assets.

- Healthcare Coverage: Health insurance covers medical expenses, providing access to quality healthcare without incurring substantial out-of-pocket costs. It helps protect against the high expenses associated with medical treatments and hospitalizations.

- Income Replacement: Life insurance and disability insurance provide income replacement for the family's beneficiaries or the insured in case of death or disability. This ensures that loved ones can maintain their financial well-being even after the loss of a breadwinner.

- Business Continuity: Business insurance protects businesses from financial losses due to disruptions, lawsuits, or property damage, ensuring the continuity and stability of the enterprise.

2. Importance of Estate Planning:

- Asset Distribution: Estate planning allows individuals to dictate how their assets will be distributed after their death. It ensures that assets are passed on to beneficiaries according to their wishes, minimizing potential conflicts among family members.

- Minimizing Taxes and Expenses: Through estate planning strategies like trusts and gifting, individuals can minimize estate taxes and probate costs, preserving more of their wealth for their heirs.

- Guardianship for Minors: Estate planning allows parents to name guardians for their minor children, ensuring they are cared for by trusted individuals if something happens to the parents.

- Healthcare Decisions: Advanced healthcare directives and living wills enable individuals to express their preferences regarding medical treatments and end-of-life care, ensuring their wishes are respected even if they are unable to communicate.

- Business Succession: For business owners, estate planning can facilitate a smooth transition of the business to the next generation or chosen successor, preserving the business's legacy and continuity.

- Avoiding Intestate Succession: Without an estate plan, assets may be distributed according to state laws (intestate succession), which may not align with an individual's wishes.

- Overall, insurance and estate planning are vital components of a comprehensive financial plan that provides protection, ensures efficient wealth transfer, and guarantees that individuals and their loved ones are cared for during times of need or transition. Seeking professional advice from insurance agents, financial advisors, and estate planning attorneys can help individuals tailor their plans to their unique circumstances and financial goals.

Mitigating Financial Risks for Peace of Mind

Mitigating financial risks is essential for achieving peace of mind and financial security. By proactively identifying potential risks and implementing risk management strategies, individuals and families can protect their assets, investments, and livelihoods from unexpected events. Insurance coverage, emergency funds, diversification of investments, and estate planning are key components in mitigating financial risks. Having a well-thought-out financial plan that addresses potential challenges can provide a sense of confidence and stability, allowing individuals to focus on their goals and aspirations without constant worry about financial uncertainties. Ultimately, by taking steps to mitigate financial risks, individuals can achieve greater peace of mind and the assurance that they are prepared for whatever life may bring

Let's consider an example of how an individual can mitigate financial risks for peace of mind:

John is a 35-year-old professional with a stable job, a mortgage, and a growing investment portfolio. He is concerned about potential financial risks that could impact his family's well-being. To achieve peace of mind, John takes the following steps to mitigate these risks:

Comprehensive Insurance Coverage: John reviews his insurance policies and ensures that he has adequate coverage for various risks. He maintains health insurance to protect against unexpected medical expenses. He also has a life insurance policy that would provide financial support to his family in case of his untimely demise. Additionally, he has home insurance to protect his property from damage or loss due to unforeseen events.

Emergency Fund: John establishes an emergency fund equal to six months' worth of living expenses. This fund provides a financial cushion in case of job loss or any other unexpected financial challenges. Having an emergency fund gives him peace of mind, knowing that he can cover essential expenses during difficult times without resorting to high-interest debt.

Diversified Investment Portfolio: John diversifies his investment portfolio across different asset classes, including stocks, bonds, and real estate. Diversification helps spread risk and reduces the impact of market volatility on his overall investments. By diversifying, John is better prepared to weather market fluctuations and safeguard his wealth.

Estate Planning: John consults with an estate planning attorney to create a comprehensive estate plan. He establishes a will, designates beneficiaries, and sets up a trust for his minor children. Through estate planning, John ensures that his assets will be distributed according to his wishes and that his loved ones are taken care of, even in his absence.

Debt Management: John manages his debt responsibly, ensuring that he does not take on excessive debt that could strain his finances. He prioritizes paying off high-interest debts and avoids taking on unnecessary loans.

By implementing these risk mitigation strategies, John gains peace of mind, knowing that he has taken proactive steps to protect his family's financial well-being. He can focus on his career and personal goals, confident that he is prepared for potential financial challenges. Mitigating financial risks allows John to navigate life's uncertainties with greater confidence and security, ultimately leading to a more peaceful and fulfilling financial journey.

CHAPTER 8

THE ART OF NEGOTIATION AND NETWORKING

Developing effective Negotiation Skills

Developing effective negotiation skills is crucial for achieving successful outcomes in various aspects of life, including business, personal relationships, and conflict resolution. Effective negotiation skills enable individuals to communicate their needs, understand others' perspectives, and find mutually beneficial solutions. Here are key steps to develop and enhance negotiation skills:

1. Preparation: Thoroughly prepare for each negotiation by researching the subject matter, understanding the interests of all

parties involved, and setting clear objectives. The more prepared you are, the more confident and assertive you can be during the negotiation process.

2. Active Listening: Actively listen to the other party's concerns, needs, and viewpoints. Paying attention and showing empathy can help build rapport and demonstrate that you value their perspective.

3. Effective Communication: Clearly and assertively communicate your position, interests, and goals. Use concise and persuasive language to express your points and avoid misunderstandings.

4. Flexibility and Creativity: Be open to compromise and explore creative solutions that can meet both parties' interests. Flexibility and creativity in problem-solving can lead to win-win outcomes.

5. Emotional Intelligence: Develop emotional intelligence to manage your emotions and recognize the emotions of others during negotiations. Being emotionally aware helps maintain a constructive atmosphere and build rapport.

6. Patience and Perseverance: Negotiations can be complex and may require time and effort. Stay patient and persevere through challenges, focusing on finding common ground and reaching a beneficial agreement.

7. Understanding Power Dynamics: Be aware of power dynamics and relationships among parties in the negotiation. Understanding power imbalances can help you navigate negotiations more effectively.

8. Building Trust: Trust is a vital element in negotiation. Be honest, reliable, and transparent to build trust with the other

party. Trust enhances the chances of reaching a successful resolution.

9. Managing Conflicts: Address conflicts calmly and constructively. Seek to understand the root causes of conflicts and work towards resolving them collaboratively.

10. Post-Negotiation Review: After the negotiation, review the outcomes and identify lessons learned. Assess your performance and areas for improvement to enhance future negotiation skills.

11. Continuous Learning: Engage in training programs, workshops, or courses that focus on negotiation skills. Learning from experts and practicing in various scenarios can sharpen your negotiation abilities.

By developing effective negotiation skills, individuals can enhance their ability to communicate, collaborate, and find solutions that meet their objectives while maintaining positive relationships with others. These skills are valuable in personal and professional settings, enabling individuals to navigate various challenges and achieve positive outcomes in a wide range of situations.

Building Strong Networks for Opportunities

Building strong networks is a powerful strategy for creating opportunities and advancing both personal and professional goals. A robust network provides access to valuable resources, information, and support from a diverse group of individuals. Here are key steps to build strong networks for opportunities:

1. Identify Your Goals: Clarify your objectives and the specific opportunities you seek. Understanding your goals helps you identify the right people and communities to connect with.

2. Attend Networking Events: Attend industry conferences, seminars, workshops, and networking events to meet like-minded individuals and professionals. These events offer valuable opportunities to connect and exchange ideas.

3. Engage in Online Networking: Utilize social media platforms and professional networking sites, such as LinkedIn, to connect with individuals in your industry or field of interest. Actively participate in relevant groups and discussions to expand your network.

4. Be Genuine and Authentic: Build relationships based on authenticity and genuine interest in others. People are more likely to connect with you when they sense sincerity in your interactions.

5. Give Before You Receive: Offer help and support to others without expecting anything in return. Be generous with your time, expertise, and resources, as it fosters a sense of reciprocity and strengthens relationships.

6. Follow Up: After meeting new contacts, follow up with them to maintain the connection. Sending personalized follow-up messages or emails shows that you value the relationship.

7. Attend Informal Gatherings: Participate in informal gatherings, such as social events or meetups, to build more personal connections with potential network partners.

8. Join Professional Associations: Become a member of relevant professional associations or organizations in your field. These

associations offer networking opportunities, educational resources, and exposure to industry trends.

9. Seek Mentors and Advisors: Look for mentors or advisors who can provide guidance and support in your career or business pursuits. Their insights and experience can be invaluable for personal growth and professional development.

10. Be Open to Diversity: Embrace diversity in your network by connecting with people from different backgrounds, industries, and experiences. A diverse network brings fresh perspectives and widens your pool of opportunities.

11. Maintain Relationships: Nurturing relationships is essential for a strong network. Regularly stay in touch with your contacts, share updates, and be responsive to their needs and interests.

By actively building and maintaining strong networks, individuals can access a wealth of opportunities, such as job openings, partnerships, collaborations, mentorship, and valuable industry insights. Strong networks provide a support system that can help individuals navigate challenges, stay informed, and capitalize on various opportunities throughout their personal and professional journey.

Collaborating and partnering for growth

Collaborating and partnering for growth is a strategic approach that allows businesses to leverage each other's strengths, resources, and expertise to achieve mutual growth and success. Through collaborations and partnerships, businesses can access new markets, expand their product or service offerings, and enhance their competitive advantage. By pooling resources and working together, organizations can tackle challenges more effectively and seize opportunities that may have been out of reach individually. Collaborations can take various forms, including joint ventures, strategic alliances, co-marketing efforts, and supplier partnerships. Successful collaborations require clear communication, shared goals, and a commitment to mutual benefit. When businesses collaborate and partner for growth, they create a synergistic environment that fosters innovation, accelerates growth, and positions them for long-term success in a competitive marketplace.

CHAPTER 9

MINDFULLNESS AND WEALTH

Balancing material Wealth and Well-being

Balancing material wealth and well-being is a delicate and essential aspect of living a fulfilling life. While material wealth can provide comfort, security, and access to various opportunities, true well-being encompasses physical, emotional, and mental health, as well as meaningful relationships and personal growth. Striking the right balance between the pursuit of material wealth and overall well-being involves several key considerations. It requires individuals to identify their core values, set clear priorities, and avoid excessive focus on accumulating possessions or wealth at the expense of health and happiness. Practicing mindfulness, gratitude, and self-awareness can help individuals appreciate non-material aspects of life and find joy in simple experiences. Cultivating a healthy work-life balance, nurturing relationships, and investing time in personal growth and self-care contribute to overall well-being. By aligning material wealth with well-being, individuals can lead more fulfilling lives, experiencing both the benefits of financial success and the richness of a life filled with purpose, happiness, and contentment

Let's consider an example of how an individual balances material wealth and well-being:

Sarah is a successful entrepreneur in her early thirties. She has built a thriving business that generates substantial profits, leading to significant material wealth. However, Sarah realizes that her relentless pursuit of financial success has taken a toll on her well-being. She often finds herself overwhelmed, stressed, and neglecting her physical health and personal relationships.

To achieve a better balance, Sarah takes the following steps:

1. Prioritizing Health and Well-being: Sarah recognizes that her well-being is essential for sustained success. She schedules regular exercise sessions, practices meditation, and ensures sufficient sleep to improve her physical and mental health.

2. Setting Boundaries: Sarah sets boundaries on her work hours and allocates time for personal activities, hobbies, and spending quality time with family and friends. She limits work-related activities during weekends to create a healthy work-life balance.

3. Practicing Mindfulness: Sarah incorporates mindfulness practices into her daily routine to stay present and appreciate life

beyond material pursuits. She cultivates gratitude for what she has achieved and finds joy in simple moments.

4. Giving Back: Recognizing the importance of giving back, Sarah allocates a portion of her wealth to charitable causes that resonate with her values. Contributing to society helps her find a sense of purpose beyond financial gains.

5. Learning and Personal Growth: Sarah invests in her personal growth by attending workshops, reading books, and seeking mentorship. This helps her develop a more well-rounded perspective on success and fulfillment.

6. Reevaluating Priorities: Sarah regularly reevaluates her priorities and aligns her business goals with her personal values. She avoids chasing material wealth solely for its own sake and focuses on ventures that align with her passions and desire to make a positive impact.

7. Seeking Support: Sarah seeks support from family, friends, and mentors during challenging times. Sharing her struggles and seeking advice helps her navigate the journey to balance material success with overall well-being.

By adopting these strategies, Sarah finds greater harmony between her material wealth and well-being. She experiences increased contentment, reduced stress, and improved overall satisfaction with her life. Striking a balance allows Sarah to enjoy the benefits of her financial success while nurturing her personal growth, health, and meaningful relationships, resulting in a more fulfilling and purpose-driven life.

Mindful spending and conscious Consumption

Mindful spending and conscious consumption are essential practices that promote financial well-being and sustainable living. Mindful spending involves being aware of our purchasing decisions, understanding the true value of the items or experiences we buy, and aligning our spending with our values and priorities. It encourages thoughtful consideration of whether a purchase is necessary and whether it contributes positively to our lives. Conscious consumption, on the other hand, involves being mindful of the impact our choices have on the environment, society, and our overall well-being. It means opting for products and services that are eco-friendly, ethically produced, and aligned with sustainable practices.

By adopting mindful spending and conscious consumption, individuals can reduce impulsive and unnecessary purchases, avoid excessive consumerism, and focus on experiences and investments that truly enhance their lives. Practicing these principles allows individuals to create a healthier relationship with money, reduce financial stress, and contribute to a more sustainable and responsible world. Mindful spending and conscious consumption also empower consumers to support businesses and brands that share their values, promoting a positive impact on society and the planet. Ultimately, embracing these practices leads to a more fulfilling and purpose-driven lifestyle that reflects our authentic selves and contributes to a more sustainable and equitable future for all.

Gratitude and Contentment in the Pursuit of Wealth

Gratitude and contentment play a vital role in the pursuit of wealth and financial success. While the desire to achieve material abundance is natural, cultivating a mindset of gratitude and contentment can positively influence the journey and the ultimate satisfaction with the outcomes. Here's how gratitude and contentment contribute to the pursuit of wealth:

1. Perspective and Fulfillment: Gratitude allows individuals to appreciate what they have achieved and the opportunities available to them. By acknowledging their current blessings, individuals can find contentment in their progress, fostering a sense of fulfillment along the way.

2. Healthy Ambition: While ambition is essential for growth, gratitude ensures that individuals maintain a healthy perspective on their goals. It prevents excessive attachment to outcomes and reduces the risk of becoming consumed by the pursuit of wealth at the expense of personal well-being.

3. Emotional Well-being: Gratitude has been linked to improved emotional well-being and reduced stress. When individuals focus on what they are grateful for, they experience greater contentment, leading to better decision-making and a more positive outlook.

4. Motivation and Positivity: Gratitude fosters a positive mindset, encouraging individuals to approach challenges with optimism and resilience. This positivity can fuel motivation, drive creativity, and inspire innovative solutions to achieve financial goals.

5. Balanced Lifestyle: Contentment helps individuals strike a balance between their pursuit of wealth and other aspects of life, such as relationships, health, and personal growth. This balance contributes to overall well-being and prevents burnout.

6. Generosity and Giving: Gratitude often leads to a desire to give back and help others. When individuals are grateful for their success, they are more likely to engage in philanthropy and

contribute to causes they care about, enriching their lives and the lives of others.

7. Humility and Openness: Gratitude fosters humility and openness to learning from others. Individuals who remain grateful for their achievements are more willing to seek advice, collaborate, and stay receptive to new ideas.

By integrating gratitude and contentment into the pursuit of wealth, individuals can create a more meaningful and fulfilling journey. These qualities promote a healthy approach to financial success, one that is balanced, grounded, and focused on holistic well-being. Embracing gratitude and contentment enables individuals to appreciate their progress, celebrate accomplishments, and savor the moments along the way, making the pursuit of wealth a rewarding and enriching experience.

CHAPTER 10

WEALTH AND HAPPINESS

Understanding the connection between Wealth and Happiness

The connection between wealth and happiness is a complex and multifaceted relationship that has been widely studied and debated. While wealth can undoubtedly provide opportunities for comfort, security, and access to various experiences, its direct correlation with happiness is not as straightforward as one might assume.

Research shows that an increase in wealth can lead to an initial boost in happiness, particularly for individuals who have experienced financial struggles. However, this effect tends to diminish over time, and there is a diminishing return on happiness as wealth continues to grow. This phenomenon is known as the "hedonic treadmill," where individuals adapt to their improved financial circumstances, and the initial happiness boost becomes less pronounced.

Happiness is influenced by various factors beyond material wealth, including social connections, meaningful relationships, personal growth, and a sense of purpose and fulfillment. While wealth can enhance certain aspects of well-being, it does not guarantee lasting happiness on its own.

Moreover, the pursuit of wealth can sometimes lead to negative consequences, such as increased stress, time constraints, and a focus on material possessions over life's more meaningful experiences. In some cases, excessive preoccupation with wealth can even erode happiness and overall life satisfaction.

However, when wealth is used wisely, it can contribute positively to happiness. Financial security and freedom can reduce stress and provide individuals with more opportunities to pursue their passions and engage in experiences that bring joy and fulfillment. Additionally, using wealth to contribute to the well-being of others through charitable giving and philanthropy can create a sense of purpose and increase happiness.

Ultimately, the connection between wealth and happiness is influenced by individual values, priorities, and how wealth is managed and utilized. Striking a balance between financial aspirations and other sources of happiness, such as meaningful relationships, personal growth, and a sense of purpose, is essential for achieving a more holistic and enduring sense of happiness and well-being.

Cultivating a Balanced and fulfilling Life

Cultivating a balanced and fulfilling life is a journey that involves aligning various aspects of life to create harmony, purpose, and overall well-being. Here are key principles and practices to achieve a balanced and fulfilling life:

1. Define Your Priorities: Clarify your core values and identify what matters most to you. Understanding your priorities helps you make decisions that align with your goals and values.

2. Work-Life Balance: Strive to strike a healthy work-life balance. Allocate time for work, family, personal growth, leisure, and self-care. Avoid excessive focus on one aspect of life at the expense of others.

3. Pursue Passions and Hobbies: Engage in activities that bring joy and fulfillment. Pursuing passions and hobbies nourishes the soul and fosters a sense of purpose beyond professional success.

4. Nurture Relationships: Cultivate meaningful relationships with family, friends, and loved ones. Spending quality time and fostering connections with others contribute to emotional well-being.

5. Practice Self-Care: Prioritize self-care and well-being. Regularly engage in activities that promote physical, emotional, and mental health, such as exercise, meditation, and adequate rest.

6. Continuous Learning and Growth: Embrace lifelong learning and personal growth. Acquiring new skills, seeking knowledge, and challenging yourself intellectually enrich your life.

7. Gratitude and Mindfulness: Practice gratitude and mindfulness to appreciate the present moment and count your blessings. Being mindful enhances awareness and contentment in daily life.

8. Limit Material Pursuits: While financial success is essential, avoid excessive materialism. Focus on experiences, relationships, and personal development rather than solely pursuing material possessions.

9. Give Back and Contribute: Engage in acts of kindness and give back to the community. Contributing to the well-being of others fosters a sense of purpose and fulfillment.

10. Set Realistic Goals: Set achievable and realistic goals for different areas of life. Celebrate progress and small victories along the way.

11. Embrace Flexibility: Embrace flexibility and adaptability. Life is dynamic, and being open to change allows you to navigate challenges and uncertainties more effectively.

12. Unplug and Reconnect with Nature: Take time to disconnect from technology and reconnect with nature. Spending time outdoors can rejuvenate the mind and soul.

Cultivating a balanced and fulfilling life involves making conscious choices that integrate various aspects of life harmoniously. It requires ongoing self-awareness, self-compassion, and a willingness to adjust priorities as life evolves. By nurturing relationships, pursuing passions, practicing gratitude, and maintaining a sense of purpose, individuals can create a more meaningful, enriching, and balanced life that aligns with their unique values and aspirations.

Finding Joy and purpose in the pursuit of wealth

Finding joy and purpose in the pursuit of wealth involves infusing meaning and positive experiences into the journey of financial success. While wealth may be a desirable goal, it is essential to recognize that true fulfillment comes not only from the end destination but also from the experiences and personal growth along the way.

To find joy in the pursuit of wealth, individuals can focus on aligning their efforts with their passions and values. By engaging in work or entrepreneurship that resonates with their interests, talents, and aspirations, they can experience a sense of purpose and fulfillment in their daily endeavors.

Moreover, finding joy in the pursuit of wealth requires celebrating milestones and achievements, no matter how small. Acknowledging progress and cherishing the positive impact of one's efforts can enhance motivation and bring a sense of accomplishment.

Additionally, individuals can cultivate gratitude and mindfulness throughout their financial journey. Appreciating the opportunities, learning experiences, and support from others can lead to a more positive and content outlook on the path to wealth.

Finding purpose in the pursuit of wealth involves recognizing how financial success can contribute to the well-being of oneself and others. By setting meaningful financial goals and linking them to broader life objectives, individuals can find purpose in their financial pursuits. This purpose-driven approach empowers individuals to make a positive impact on their lives, the lives of loved ones, and the community.

Ultimately, the key to finding joy and purpose in the pursuit of wealth lies in integrating a holistic view of success, where financial achievements are complemented by personal growth, meaningful relationships, and a positive impact on society. Embracing this perspective allows individuals to derive greater satisfaction and fulfillment throughout their journey to financial success.

In conclusion, **"The Art of Wealth"** is a journey that transcends mere financial success. It is a holistic approach that emphasizes the harmonious integration of material prosperity, well-being, and a purposeful life. Throughout this book, we have explored various principles, strategies, and mindsets that contribute to building true wealth – one that encompasses financial abundance, emotional well-being, and meaningful relationships.

We have learned that cultivating a balanced and fulfilling life involves aligning our values, setting clear goals, and making conscious choices that prioritize personal growth and the well-being of ourselves and others. By practicing gratitude, mindfulness, and self-awareness, we can find joy and purpose in the pursuit of wealth, celebrating not only the destination but also the transformative journey.

"The Art of Wealth" encourages us to recognize that wealth extends beyond material possessions; it resides in experiences, in giving back to the community, and in making a positive impact on the world. By nurturing our relationships, pursuing our passions, and staying open to learning and growth, we can create a life rich in meaning and contentment.

As we apply the principles outlined in this book, let us remember that wealth is not an end in itself, but a means to live a life of purpose, abundance, and contribution. Let us embrace the art of wealth as an ongoing practice, one that enriches our lives and empowers us to create a better world for ourselves and those around us.

May **"The Art of Wealth"** serve as a guiding light on your journey to financial prosperity, well-being, and fulfillment? May it inspire you to lead a life that blends financial success with personal growth and lasting happiness? As you embark on this path, remember that true wealth lies not only in what you accumulate but also in the joy of giving, the value of meaningful connections, and the fulfillment of living with purpose. Here's to a life well-lived – a life truly abundant in every sense.

Thanks